Animal Young

Mammals

Revised and updated

Rod Theodorou

www.heinemann.co.uk/library
Visit our website to find out more information about Heinemann Library books.

To order:
☎ Phone 44 (0) 1865 888066
Send a fax to 44 (0) 1865 314091
📄 Visit the Heinemann Bookshop at www.heinemann.co.uk/library to browse our
💻 catalogue and order online.

First published in Great Britain by Heinemann Library,
Halley Court, Jordan Hill, Oxford OX2 8EJ, part
of Harcourt Education. Heinemann is a registered
trademark of Harcourt Education Ltd.

Editorial: Clare Lewis
Design: Joanna Hinton-Malivoire
Illustration: Barry Atkinson Illustration
Picture research: Ruth Blair
Production: Sevy Ribierre

Printed and bound in China by South
China Printing Co. Ltd.

10-digit ISBN 0 431 93236 0
13-digit ISBN 978 0 431 93236 1
11 10 09 08 07
10 9 8 7 6 5 4 3 2 1

British Library Cataloguing in Publication Data
Theodorou, Rod
Animal Young: Mammals – 2nd edition
599.1'39
A full catalogue record for this book is available from
the British Library.

Acknowledgements
The publishers would like to thank the following for
permission to reproduce photographs:
Alamy: Brandon Cole Marine Photography p. **21**; Ardea:
Brian Bevan p. **30**, John Daniels p. **9**; BBC: Andrew
Cooper p. **10**, John Cancalosi p. **15**, Anup Shah p.
17, Thomas D Magelsen p. **23**; Bruce Coleman: Jane
Burton p. **6**, Rod Williams p. **13**; Creatas p. **4** bottom
left; Digital Stock p. **4** top right and middle left; Digital
Vision p. **4** bottom right; Frank Lane: Silvestris p. **11**;
Jupiter Images / Stock Image p. **25**; Getty Images p. **4**
top left and middle right; NHPA: A.N.T. p. **7**, Ernie Janes
pp. **12**, **20**, Gerard Lacz p. **22**, Michael Leach p. **24**;
OSF: Richard Kolar p. **8**, Martyn Colbeck
p. **16**, Owen Newman p. **19**; Tony Stone: Renee Lynn
p. **5**, Art Wolfe p. **14**, Norbert Wu p. **18**.

Cover photograph of a hippo with young
reproduced with permission of NHPA/Ann & Steve
Toon.

Every effort has been made to contact copyright holders
of any material reproduced in this book. Any omissions
will be rectified in subsequent printings if notice is given
to the publishers.

Contents

Introduction 4

What is a mammal? 6

Birth 8

Looking after baby 10

Feeding 12

Moving about 14

Family life 16

Brothers and sisters 18

Learning from parents 20

Learning to feed. 22

Leaving home 24

Mammal life cycles 26

Mammals and other animals 28

Marvellous mammals! 30

Glossary 31

Find out more 32

Index 32

Some words are shown in bold, **like this**. You can find out what they mean by looking in the Glossary.

Introduction

There are many different types of animals. All animals have babies. They look after their babies in different ways.

These are the six main animal groups.

Mammal

Bird

Amphibian

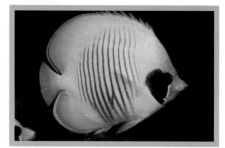
Fish

Reptile

Insect

Orangutans are mammals.
They live in rainforests.

This book is about mammals. Some
mammals are tiny. Some mammals are
huge. Mammals live all over the world.

What is a mammal?

All mammals:

- breathe air
- feed their young milk from **teats** on the mother's body
- have hair on their bodies.

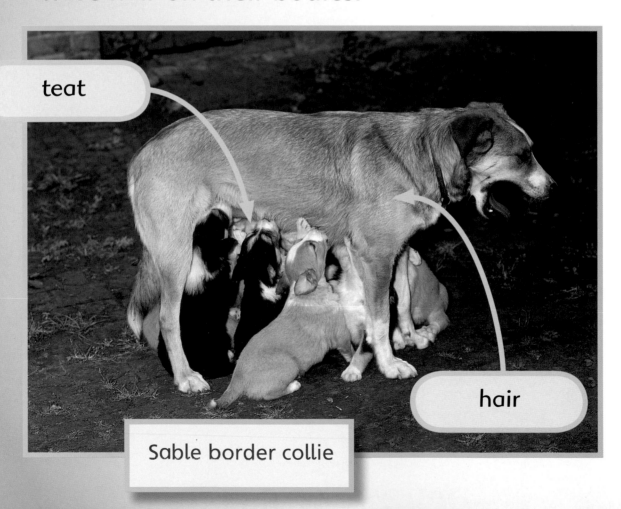

teat

hair

Sable border collie

Most mammals:

- grow babies inside the mother's body
- give birth to live babies
- live on land and walk on four legs.

Platypus babies **hatch** from eggs, but they are mammals too!

1

Birth

Some mammal mothers have one baby at a time. Others have lots of babies at once. Most mammals look for a safe place to have their babies.

Mice can have more than 15 babies in one **litter**.

Kittens are born blind. Their eyes open when they are about nine days old.

Some mammal babies are born blind. Their parents look after them until their eyes open. Other mammal babies can see and run with their parents very soon after they are born.

Looking after baby

Most mammals take care of their babies. Small mammals build burrows or nests for them to live in. They bring them food until they are old enough to find their own.

This mother fox has dug a burrow in the ground to keep her babies safe and warm.

Some mammals have to keep moving to find food or keep out of danger. Some carry their babies by the scruff of the neck. Other babies hold on to their mothers.

This baby bat holds onto its mother even when she is flying.

baby bat

Feeding

Mother mammals feed their babies milk from their **teats**. The milk helps the babies grow quickly.

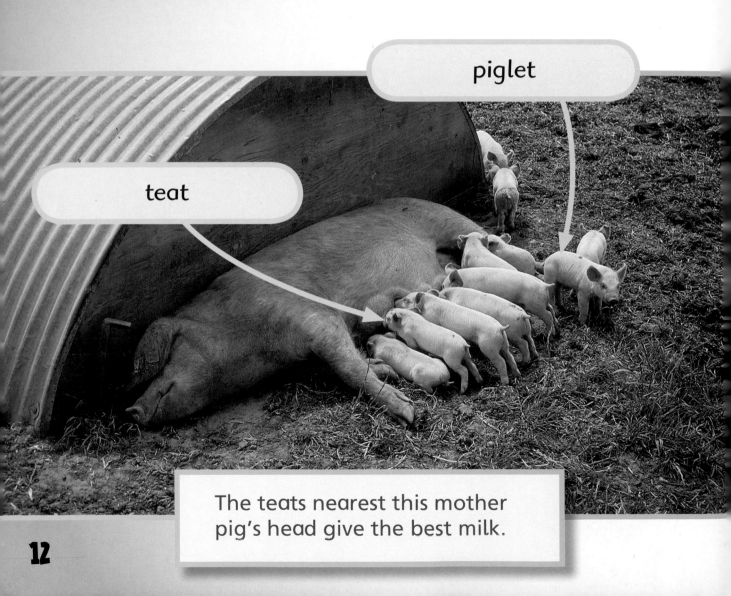

piglet

teat

The teats nearest this mother pig's head give the best milk.

These snow leopard babies are waiting for their mother to bring them meat.

Mammals need lots of food for energy and warmth. As the babies get older, their mothers **wean** them off milk. The babies have to start eating solid food.

13

Moving about

Some mammal babies can move around soon after they are born. They learn to walk or run so they can escape from **predators** and follow their parents.

Baby giraffes have to stand up and run soon after they are born.

Joeys leave their mother's
pouch when they are about
nine months old. They jump
back in if they are scared
or hungry.

pouch

Other mammal babies cannot walk or
run when they are born. They stay close
to their mother while they grow bigger
and stronger.

Family life

Many mammals live in large family groups, called **herds**. They help each other look after the young and **protect** them from danger.

When the herd go to look for food, some female elephants stay behind to "babysit" all the young elephants.

Mothers in a herd always know which are their babies by their look, smell, and call. They spend a lot of time **grooming** and cleaning the babies.

Chimpanzee mothers pick dirt and insects out of their babies' hair.

Brothers and sisters

When they are young, most mammals spend a lot of time with their **siblings**, especially if they live in a **herd** or family group.

Young dolphins swim with their siblings. They may even fight young dolphins from other groups.

This game will help these lion cubs
learn to hunt and catch food.

Brothers and sisters sometimes have play
fights. This helps them grow stronger. It is
also good practice for fighting **predators**
or for hunting **prey**.

Learning from parents

Some mammal babies have very good **instincts**. They do not have to learn everything from their parents. They know how to find food and look out for danger.

A young mouse knows how to find food and stay hidden from **predators**.

Other mammals have to learn some things from their parents. Some remember how their mothers looked after them, so they can look after their own babies.

Whale calves can swim as soon as they are born, but their mother has to push them to the surface to teach them to breathe air.

baby whale

Learning to feed

Many mammals teach their babies to hunt or find food. Hunting mammals sometimes bring small or **injured** animals back to their young so they can learn how to attack.

This tiger mother teaches her cubs how to hunt other animals.

These bear cubs watch carefully to see how their mother catches fish.

Some baby mammals spend a lot of time watching how their mother finds food. They will remember what plants are good to eat or what animals are easy to catch.

Leaving home

Some mammal babies take years to grow up. Others grow up very quickly. Once they have grown up, mammals **mate** to have babies of their own.

Voles are ready to have their own babies when they are only 15 days old.

Humans are mammals too. We look after our young for longer than any other mammals.

When they are old enough, some mammals leave their mother and find a new place to live. Others stay with their **herd** all their lives.

Mammal life cycles

This is how a baby lion grows up.

1. The baby lion grows inside its mother.

2. The mother gives birth and feeds her cub milk.

3. The cub grows bigger. Its mother brings food for it to eat.

4. The young lion learns to hunt.

5. The young lion is nearly fully-grown. It can hunt for food.

This is how a baby whale grows up.

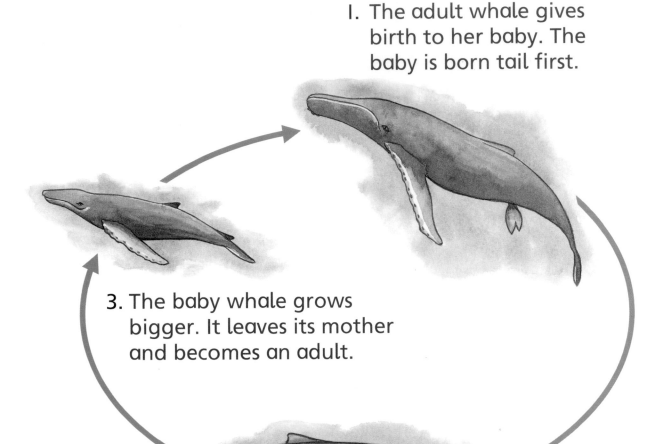

1. The adult whale gives birth to her baby. The baby is born tail first.

3. The baby whale grows bigger. It leaves its mother and becomes an adult.

2. The baby whale drinks milk from its mother.

27

Mammals and other animals

		MAMMALS	
WHAT THEY LOOK LIKE:	Bones inside body	all	
	Number of legs	none, 2, or 4	
	Hair on body	all	
	Scaly skin	few	
	Wings	some	
	Feathers	none	
WHERE THEY LIVE:	On land	most	
	In water	some	
HOW THEY ARE BORN:	Grows babies inside body	most	
	Lays eggs	few	
HOW THEY FEED YOUNG:	Feeds baby milk	all	
	Brings baby food	most	

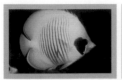 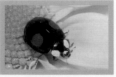   

FISH	INSECTS	AMPHIBIANS	BIRDS	REPTILES
all	none	all	all	all
none	6	4 or none	2	4 or none
none	all	none	none	none
most	none	none	none	all
none	most	none	all	none
none	none	none	all	none
none	most	most	all	most
all	some	some	none	some
some	some	few	none	some
most	most	most	all	most
none	none	none	none	none
none	some	none	most	none

29

Marvellous mammals!

- Dolphins and whales look like fish, but they are really mammals. They even have some hair on their bodies, but this can be hard to see.

- The biggest mammal is the blue whale. A newborn baby blue whale is as big as a car!

- The smallest mammal is the pygmy shrew. Even when it is fully grown, it only weighs as much as a paperclip!

Pygmy shrew

Glossary

grooming to keep healthy by cleaning and brushing fur or hair

hatch to be born from an egg

herd large group of animals of one kind that live together

injured hurt

instinct to be able to do something without being told how to

joey a baby kangaroo

litter group of animals that are born at the same time and have the same mother

mate when a male and a female animal come together to make babies

pouch pocket of skin on the stomach of some animals in which their babies grow

predator an animal that hunts and kills other animals for food

prey an animal that is hunted by another for food

protect to look after

sibling brother or sister

teat part of a female animal's body which the babies suck to get milk

wean when a baby animal stops feeding on its mother's milk and eats other food

Find out more

Books

How Living Things Grow: From Puppy to Dog, Anita Ganeri (Heinemann Library, 2006)

Save our Animals! Save the Blue Whale, Louise and Richard Spilsbury (Heinemann Library, 2006)

Wild World: Watching Lions in Africa, Louise and Richard Spilsbury (Heinemann Library, 2006)

Website

www.bbc.co.uk/nature/reallywild/

Index

animal groups 4

babies 7, 8, 9, 10, 11, 12, 13, 14, 15, 17, 20, 21, 22, 24, 26, 27

eggs 7

food 10, 11, 12, 13, 16, 19, 20, 22, 23, 26, 27

games 19

grooming 17

hair 6, 17

herds 16, 17, 18, 25

instincts 20

litters 8

nests 10

pouch 15

predators 14, 19, 20

siblings 18

teats 6, 12

Titles in the *Animal Young* series include:

Hardback   978-0-431-93232-3

Hardback   978-0-431-93233-0

Hardback   978-0-431-93234-7

Hardback   978-0-431-93235-4

Hardback   978-0-431-93236-1

Hardback   978-0-431-93237-8

Find out about other titles from Heinemann Library on our website www.heinemann.co.uk/library